What Did We Do?

Before Social Media

by Susan E. Hamen

T0015102

FOCUS
READERS.

BEACON

www.focusreaders.com

Focus Readers is distributed by North Star Editions:
sales@northstareditions.com | 888-417-0195

Produced for Focus Readers by Red Line Editorial.

Photographs ©: Everett Collection/Shutterstock Images, cover (left), 1 (left), 8; tum3123/Shutterstock Images, cover (right), 1 (right); jldeines/iStockphoto, 4; sirtravelalot/Shutterstock Images, 6, 29; Sergei Kolesnikov/Shutterstock Images, 11; Golden Sikorka/Shutterstock Images, 12; Everett Historical/Shutterstock Images, 14; Ruta Production/Shutterstock Images, 17; SAPhotog/Shutterstock Images, 18; Photo Love/Shutterstock Images, 20; benjamas11/Shutterstock Images, 22–23; sitthiphong/Shutterstock Images, 24; RyanJLane/iStockphoto, 27

Library of Congress Cataloging-in-Publication Data
Names: Hamen, Susan E., author.
Title: Before social media / Susan E. Hamen.
Description: Lake Elmo, MN : Focus Readers, 2020. | Series: What did we do?
  | Includes index. | Audience: Grades 4-6
Identifiers: LCCN 2019031725 (print) | LCCN 2019031726 (ebook) | ISBN
  9781644930441 (hardcover) | ISBN 9781644931233 (paperback) | ISBN
  9781644932810 (ebook pdf) | ISBN 9781644932025 (hosted ebook)
Subjects: LCSH: Communication--Juvenile literature. |
  Communication--Technological innovations--Juvenile literature.
Classification: LCC P91.2 .H265 2020 (print) | LCC P91.2 (ebook) | DDC
  [Fic]--dc23
LC record available at https://lccn.loc.gov/2019031725
LC ebook record available at https://lccn.loc.gov/2019031726

Printed in the United States of America
Mankato, MN
012020

About the Author

Susan E. Hamen is the author of more than 30 books for children. She lives in Minnesota with her husband, daughter, and son. She loves traveling with her family and keeping in touch with her friends all over the United States and Europe through social media.

Table of Contents

Chapter 1

New Friends

Sarah was nine years old in 1988. In July, she went to summer camp for the first time. She stayed in a cabin with seven other girls. Sarah had never met them before. They all came from different towns.

 Kids often stay in cabins at summer camps.

➤ **Before social media, friends often sent messages to one another by mail.**

The girls became good friends.

They did crafts. They went on hikes.

They swam in the lake.

On the last day of camp, the

girls were sad to leave. But they

agreed to write letters. They traded addresses. They sent mail to one another all year long.

Before long, summer arrived. The girls packed their bags for camp. They were excited to be together again. And they were glad they had stayed in touch by writing letters.

Fun Fact

In 1988, mailing a letter in the United States cost 25 cents.

Chapter 2

Connecting with Friends

Social media lets people **interact** online. Before social media, people mostly interacted in person. They met up to talk or play. As a result, kids usually made friends with people who lived nearby.

 Like they do today, kids in the past often got together to play games.

Sometimes they just walked over to the other person's house.

In the past, kids couldn't get instant updates from their friends online. But they communicated in other ways. Friends often called each other on the phone. Kids dialed a friend's phone number.

Fun Fact

Before cell phones, most homes had a single phone line. That meant only one person could talk on the phone at a time.

 For many years, most phones connected to the wall with a cord.

They hoped the friend was home. If not, they left a message. Then they waited for the friend to call back.

If a friend moved away, people often sent mail. They wrote letters.

STEPS IN SENDING A LETTER

One friend places the letter in a mailbox.

The letter arrives at the mail sorting station and is placed on a mail truck.

The truck carries the letter to another town.

A mail carrier delivers the letter to the other friend's house.

The letter arrives at the town's post office and is sorted for delivery.

They used stamps and envelopes to send them. The mail could take days to reach the other person.

Many friends sent mail even if they lived nearby. Kids also wrote notes on scraps of paper. They gave them to friends at school. Some kids passed notes in class. But they had to be careful not to get caught. The teacher might ask them to read the notes out loud!

People still call and send mail today. But it is much less common.

Fun Fact

Some kids write letters to people they have never met. These friends are called pen pals.

Chapter 3

Sharing Ideas

Before social media, people had other ways to find and share ideas. For example, people **subscribed** to magazines. New **issues** came in the mail. Kids read about sports, music, nature, or other hobbies.

 A man sells magazines and newspapers in New York City in the early 1900s.

Kids often shared the magazines with their friends. Of course, kids still do this today. But many people now use social media instead.

For most of the 1900s, people got news from newspapers or the radio. In the 1940s, television news programs began. Reporters filmed events and talked about what was going on around the world.

By the late 1900s, some families owned video cameras. They could now film birthdays, holidays, and

> **A man uses a video camera to film an event.**

other special events. Many video cameras used **cassettes**. People needed a VCR to watch them. This device showed the video on the TV screen. Usually, only the family saw these videos.

 People had to take rolls of film to a photo lab before they could see the pictures.

Like today, people took pictures of trips or events. But they used a much different process to share them. Early cameras used rolls of film. Each roll of film took a limited number of pictures. Some rolls had room for only 12 to 24 pictures.

After taking pictures, people brought the film to a photo lab. There, workers printed the pictures. It could take several days. Until the pictures came back, people weren't sure what the pictures looked like.

Digital cameras became common in the 1990s. They don't use film.

Fun Fact

Polaroid cameras don't use rolls of film. Instead, photos come out of the camera one at a time. Each photo **develops** in just a few seconds.

 With a memory card, people can easily move photos from a digital camera to a computer.

People no longer have to print

their pictures to see or share them.

Instead, the pictures show up on

the camera's screen. People can

save the photos on computers. They can print them at home, too.

In the 1990s, many people began using the internet. They started sending emails. Some emails shared photos. Chain mail was also popular. These emails asked people to send them to many others. Some had questions to answer. Others had fun facts or pictures. People sent each email to a group of friends. Then, those friends shared it with even more people.

Teen Magazines

Many kids love learning about celebrities. They want to know all about their favorite actors and singers. Today, kids often follow these stars on social media. In the past, kids read teen magazines. These magazines had articles about famous people.

In the 1980s, many kids read a magazine called *Tiger Beat. Seventeen* was also popular. Kids read **interviews** with stars. They also looked at photos. Kids often cut out pictures of their favorite stars. Some kids hung them on their bedroom walls. Others taped the pictures to their lockers at school.

Teen magazines tell facts about famous people.

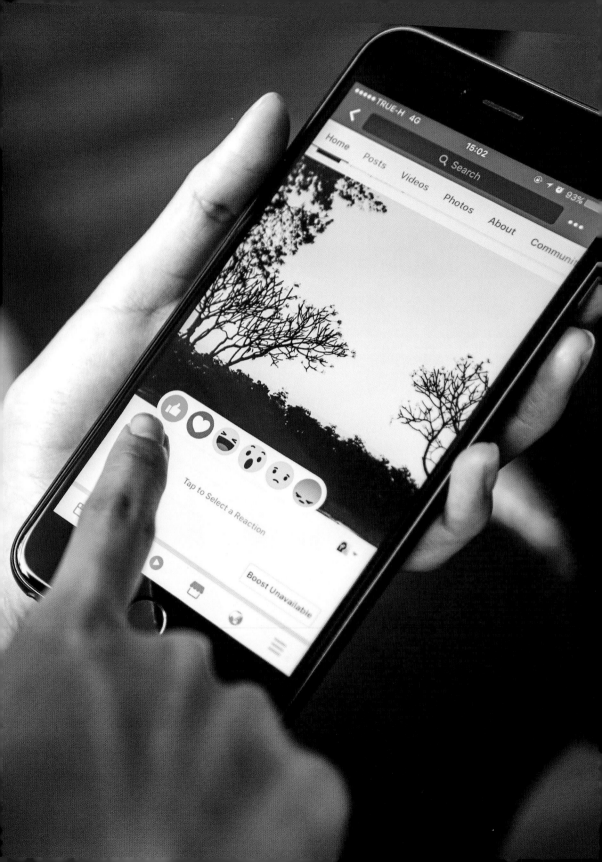

Chapter 4

Technology Today

Today, social media gives people fast and easy ways to connect. People use many **apps**. Some apps send photos or messages. Others let people video chat. Friends who live far apart can stay in touch.

 Using social media, people can see and respond to posts from others.

People can even find new friends who have similar interests.

Social media lets people share their thoughts. People post pictures and videos of what they're doing. They also share links to posts they like. Many people see each post right away.

Fun Fact

More than half of children and teens in the United States have their own social media accounts.

 Social media makes it easy for friends to share photos, videos, and messages.

Some people use social media to get news. People often post about events that happen where they live. It can be hard to tell if the posts are **accurate**. But they give people more information than ever before.

Before Social Media

Write your answers on a separate piece of paper.

1. Write a sentence describing one of the ways friends communicated before social media.

2. Do you think social media is a good way to get news? Why or why not?

3. Before social media, how did most kids find friends?

    A. by meeting people online

    B. by meeting people who lived nearby

    C. by seeing people who lived far away

4. How did digital cameras make photos easier to share?

    A. People didn't have to print copies.

    B. People didn't need to use a computer.

    C. People didn't take as many photos.

5. What does **limited** mean in this book?

*Each roll of film took a **limited** number of pictures. Some rolls had room for only 12 to 24 pictures.*

    A. only a certain amount

    B. as many as possible

    C. an unknown number

6. What does **celebrities** mean in this book?

*Many kids love learning about **celebrities**. They want to know all about their favorite actors and singers.*

    A. friends and family

    B. famous people

    C. very tall people

Answer key on page 32.

Glossary

accurate
Having correct details and no mistakes.

apps
Computer programs that complete specific tasks.

cassettes
Small cases holding magnetic tape that can be used to record sounds and images.

develops
Goes through a process to make the image in a photo visible.

digital
Having to do with information used on a computer.

interact
To talk or spend time with another person.

interviews
Conversations or stories where one person asks questions and another person answers them.

issues
Versions of a magazine or newspaper that are released at certain times.

subscribed
Signed up to receive a product or a service.

To Learn More

BOOKS

Dell, Pamela. *Understanding Social Media*. North Mankato, MN: Capstone Press, 2019.

Gregory, Josh. *Posting on Social Media.* New York: Children's Press, 2019.

Mattern, Joanne. *Instagram.* Minneapolis: Abdo Publishing, 2017.

NOTE TO EDUCATORS

Visit **www.focusreaders.com** to find lesson plans, activities, links, and other resources related to this title.

Index

Answer Key: 1. Answers will vary; 2. Answers will vary; 3. B; 4. A; 5. A; 6. B